Heinemann
LIBRARY

Scott Ingram

www.heinemann.co.uk/library
Visit our website to find out more information about **Heinemann Library** books.

To order:
☎ Phone 44 (0) 1865 888066
▤ Send a fax to 44 (0) 1865 314091
▧ Visit the Heinemann Bookshop at www.heinemann.co.uk/library to browse our catalogue and order online.

First published in Great Britain by Heinemann Library, Halley Court, Jordan Hill, Oxford OX2 8EJ, part of Harcourt Education.
Heinemann is a registered trademark of Harcourt Education Ltd.

Editorial: Geoff Barker, Rebecca Hunter and Dan Nunn
Design: Keith Williams
Illustrations: Peter Bull and Stefan Chabluk
Picture Research: Rachel Tisdale
Consultant: Simon Yeend
Production: Duncan Gilbert

Originated by Ambassador Litho Ltd
Printed in China by WKT Company Limited

ISBN 0 431 18938 2 (hardback)
08 07 06 05 04
10 9 8 7 6 5 4 3 2 1

ISBN 0 431 18948 X (paperback)
09 08 07 06 05
10 9 8 7 6 5 4 3 2 1

British Library Cataloguing in Publication Data
Ingram, William Scott
A basketball all-star – (The making of a champion)
1.Basketball – Juvenile literature
2. Basketball – Training – Juvenile literature
I. Title
796.3'23

A full catalogue record for this book is available from the British Library.

Acknowledgements
The publishers would like to thank the following for permission to reproduce photographs:

Corbis pp **7** (Hulton Deutsch Collection), **10** (Bettman), **12** (Richard Hamilton), **16** (Jose Luis Pelaez), **17 top** (Michael Cole), **19** (Catherine Wessell), **23 bottom** (Jose Luiz Pelaez); Empics pp **5 bottom**, **11**, **15 bottom**, **17 bottom**, **22**, **31 bottom**, **37 right** (Hans Deryk), **38**, **40**, **41 top**; Getty Images pp **4** (Noren Trotman), **5 top** (Ron Turenne), **6**, **8** (Jeff Haynes), **9** (Ron Koch/NBAE), **15 top** (Aris Messinis), **14** (Jesse Garrabrant/NBAE), **18** (Brian Bahr), **20** (Nathaniel Butler/NBAE), **21** (Joe Murphy/NBAE), **23 top** (Jon Buckle), **25 top** (Jesse Garrabrant/NBAE), **25 bottom** (Andy Lyons), **26** (Mladen Antonov), **27** (Jeff Reinking), **28** (Jonathan Daniel), **29 left** (Stephen Dunn), **29 right** (Rocky Widner/WNBAE), **30** (Jesse Garrabrant/NBAE), **31 top** (Jeff Reinking/WNBAE), **32** (Michael Steele), **33** (Fernando Medina), **34** (Andrew D. Bernstein/NBAE), **35 top** (Matthew Stockman), **35 bottom** (Ezra Shaw), **36** (Roy Hoskins), **37 left** (Jesse Garrabrant/NBAE), **39** (Elsa), **41 bottom** (Ron Hoskins/NBAE), **42** (Jesse Garrabrant/NBAE), **43 top** (Sam Forencich), **43 bottom** (Adam Pretty).

Cover photograph reproduced with permission of Lucy Nicholson/Reuters.

Every effort has been made to contact copyright holders of any material reproduced in this book. Any omissions will be rectified in subsequent printings if notice is given to the publishers.

The paper used to print this book comes from sustainable resources.

Contents

Words printed in bold letters, **like these**, are explained in the Glossary.

A worldwide sport

Few sports have the international appeal of basketball. It began in 1891 as a way for young men to exercise indoors during cold winter months, and has grown into the second most popular sport in the world. Now, basketball is played year-round virtually anywhere there is a flat area and a place to set up a hoop. It is played not just by young men but by boys and girls of all ages. Although a person who is tall may have an advantage, the sport welcomes players of all sizes. Basketball tests a player's athletic abilities to run, jump and handle a ball. More than that, it challenges a player's desire to improve.

International growth

For much of the twentieth century, the USA was widely acknowledged as the country that produced the best basketball players. It was, after all, the nation where the sport was invented and the home of the National Basketball Association (NBA), widely considered the best professional basketball league in the world. The popularity of the sport, however, has spread around the world. As a result, other nations now produce some of the NBA's best players.

In 2003, NBA teams featured 65 international players from 34 countries and territories, the largest foreign representation ever. Among these were the NBA's **Most Valuable Player**, Tim Duncan of the US Virgin Islands; the NBA **Rookie of the Year**, Pau Gasol from Spain; and 2003 NBA All-Stars Zydrunas Ilgauskas of Lithuania, Steve Nash of Canada, Dirk Nowitzki of Germany and Peja Stojakovic of Serbia & Montenegro.

When NBA teams held their annual meeting to choose the most promising players for professional careers, the first player selected was an 18-year-old American

Over the past five years, European players, such as Zydrunas Ilgauskas of Lithuania, have become major stars in the National Basketball Association. In 2003, more than 25 percent of the top 20 players chosen by NBA teams were from Europe, an all-time high.

Yao Ming

Perhaps the most famous international player to make his way to the NBA in recent years is Yao Ming of China. Yao, who is 2.4 metres tall, was a superstar for the national team in his homeland. His height and long arms prevented opponents from getting shots at the basket. Chinese basketball fans called him 'The Great Wall' after China's famous landmark. In 2002, Yao became the first international player to be the top choice in the NBA draft. The Houston Rockets signed Yao to a contract worth millions of dollars.

high school student from Ohio, LeBron James. Six of the next twenty selections, however, were international players, the highest number of foreign players ever chosen at that time for the premier professional league.

Basketball fact

In slightly more than a century basketball has evolved into a sport played by more than 300 million people in 144 countries. Although there are certain differences, most of the basic rules are the same around the world.

LeBron James, an 18-year-old high school student was the first player chosen in the 2003 NBA draft. James was one of the first American players to skip playing for a college team and move directly to a professional team.

Basketball beginnings

In December 1891, the New England city of Springfield, Massachusetts in the USA, was the home of the International YMCA Training School. There, Dr Luther Gulick, head of Physical Education at the school, gave their 30-year-old physical education instructor, Canadian Dr James Naismith, two weeks to create an indoor game for his class of eighteen young men. In those two weeks, the sport of basketball was invented.

Early game

The sport of 'basket ball' as it was first called had few similarities to the sport today. Naismith designed the game for nine players on each side. Players passed or batted the ball to each other with an open hand. Instead of an iron rim with a nylon net, his basket was actually a peach basket. After a basket was scored, which counted for one point, play halted while the round, soccer-sized ball was retrieved. The only similarity to today's game of basketball was the basic object of the game: throwing a ball into a goal suspended above the floor.

Native Americans played a sport that resembled basketball in which they threw a ball at a target on top of a pole. Canadian James Naismith, however, was the first to attach a basket and establish a regulation height for the pole.

Male college athletes also took up the sport. The first five-player college basketball men's game was played in 1896, at Iowa City, Iowa, where the University of Chicago defeated the University of Iowa. In 1939 – the year of Naismith's death – the first national championship game was played at Madison Square Garden in New York City.

Women's basketball began shortly after men's basketball. For both sexes, tall players have an advantage, as this photo from the early 1900s demonstrates.

The height of the goal has also remained the same since the first game – ten feet (3.05 metres).

On 21 December 1891, the first game of 'basket ball' was played. It was a contest remembered later for confusion over the rules and many **fouls**. The final score was 1–0.

Immediate popularity

Basketball was slightly more than a month old when women on the staff at the Springfield YMCA formed teams made up of secretaries and teachers' wives. The women's game also spread quickly to college campuses. The first women's teams, which had nine to eleven players, were formed in 1895 at Smith College in nearby Northampton, Massachusetts.

The growth of the NBA

The first National Basketball Association game was played on 1 November 1946 in Toronto, Canada, between the Toronto Huskies and the New York Knickerbockers. A crowd of slightly more than 7000 fans attended. Any fan taller than the 2-metre centre of the Knicks was admitted for free.

Global players

Today, the players are taller, the crowds larger, and the original six-team league has grown to 29 teams. The NBA has become the premier professional basketball league in the world. NBA players come from North America, Asia, Africa, Australia, Europe and South America. From its modest beginnings, professional basketball has achieved a global reach.

The first professional (pro) game was played in 1896 between the Trenton Basketball Team and the Brooklyn YMCA. The Trenton players triumphed, and each player was paid US$15. Early pro teams played in local leagues until World War One began in 1914.

The NBA championship now draws millions of viewers around the world. In this play from the 2003 championship, Richard Jefferson (left) of the New Jersey Nets tries to take the ball from guard Tony Parker of the San Antonio Spurs.

The influence of Julius Erving

No player did more in the 1970s to make basketball a fan favourite than Julius Erving of the ABA's New York Nets. Known as 'Doctor J' because, fans said, he could cure any team's problems, the 1.98 metres-tall Erving left college and turned pro at the age of 20 in 1971. In the five years before the two leagues merged, Erving was voted the **Most Valuable Player** in the ABA for three consecutive seasons and led the ABA in scoring averages three times. In 1976, when the ABA and NBA merged, Erving's contract was sold to the Philadelphia 76ers of the NBA. There he continued his success, winning the NBA's Most Valuable Player Award in 1981 and leading the 76ers to the NBA championship in 1982. With 30,026 career points in both leagues, Erving is third on the all-time professional scoring list.

In 1945, the first financially successful professional league, the Basketball Association of America (BAA), was formed. In 1949, the president of the BAA, persuaded twelve big-city teams to join with teams from the National Basketball League, a small league in the Midwest, to form the National Basketball Association (NBA). Throughout the 1950s and 1960s, the NBA was dominated by one team: the Boston Celtics, which won eleven world championships in thirteen years.

American Basketball Association (ABA)

In 1967, a new professional league, the American Basketball Association (ABA), was founded to compete with the NBA. At that time, the 10-team NBA had only 120 players. Many excellent players were overlooked because the NBA had a rule that its players had to graduate from college. To compete for top players, the ABA declared that a player did not have

to be a college graduate. As a result, many college players went into the ABA before graduating. Recruitment of players before graduation was one of the great steps forward in professional basketball.

In June 1976, the rival pro leagues merged. Four of the strongest ABA teams, the New York Nets, Denver Nuggets, Indiana Pacers and San Antonio Spurs, joined the NBA. In 2003, the NBA finals were played between two former ABA teams. The San Antonio Spurs defeated the New Jersey (formerly New York) Nets to win the world championship.

Changes in the rules

As more and more athletes began to choose basketball over other sports, the quality of play improved and rules were developed to address players' athletic skills. The best players developed shooting and ballhandling innovations. Taller players with athletic gifts caused the rules of the game to change.

The jump shot

In early basketball, the most common shot was the set shot. To execute this shot, a player remained stationary, both feet planted on the floor. Holding the ball with hands on either side, the player pushed the ball toward the basket. Eventually, players began to take a one-handed set shot in which they placed one hand under the ball and one hand behind it, fingers pointing toward the basket, and shot while 'set' (stationary) on the floor. The change in hand position led to the next great evolution in shooting, the jump shot. That shot was basically a shot with hands behind and below the ball taken while the player jumped above the defender.

Ballhandling

From basketball's earliest days, the job of dribbling the ball from one end of the court to the other fell to the players in the **guard** position. Because the original rules forbid anyone who dribbled the ball from shooting, players who handled the ball had to not only dribble well but pass accurately. In general, these were the players known as guards. In most cases, fans were more interested in accurate shooters and tall defenders. As the speed of the sport increased, however, guards took on added importance. **Centres** had to receive the ball at the right

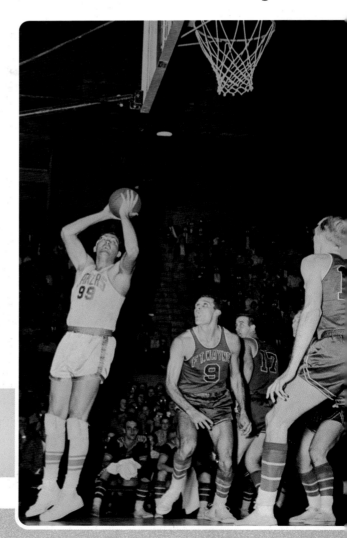

At 2.08 metres tall, George Mikan (left) was the first 'giant' in college and professional basketball. His ability to block opponents' shots close to the basket led to an important change in the rules of the game.

height to be able to shoot without shorter players grabbing at the ball. **Forwards**, the most athletic of the bigger players, had to receive accurate passes while they ran at full speed.

Changed rules

From the early days of basketball, tall players – known as centres on the court – had an advantage. On defence, taller men could block the vision or shots of shorter players. As a result, teams positioned their tallest players near the basket. From that spot, they simply swatted away shots around the basket in the same way that a soccer goalkeeper might block shots. As the game evolved, big

Goaltending differences fact

At all levels of basketball it is against the rules to stop a shot on its downward path. In the NBA and other professional leagues it is also forbidden for a player to trap a ball against the backboard to prevent it from bouncing into the basket, no matter what direction the ball is travelling. In collegiate and international rules a defender is allowed to pin a shot against the backboard to prevent it from bouncing into the basket.

men who were athletically skilled were able to jump high above the basket to create an almost impenetrable barrier for smaller shooters. To ensure that taller players did not have an unfair advantage, basketball developed the goaltending rule. This rule stated that a player could not block a shot on its downward path to the basket.

Bob Cousy was one of basketball's first players to use behind-the-back and 'no-look' passes for the Boston Celtics in the 1950s.

Basketball basics

Wherever basketball is played, no matter what the level, the basic foundation of the game remains the same. All teams have five players on the court: one **centre**, two **forwards**, and two **guards**. A game begins when a referee tosses up a jump ball at the circle in the middle of the court, called centre court. In most cases, the tallest players, usually the centres, jump for possession of the ball. The object of the game is to score more points than the opponent.

The game

College and international games are 40 minutes long, played either in two 20-minute halves or in four 10-minute quarters. Professional (NBA) games are 48 minutes long, played in four 12-minute quarters. At the mid-point or half of each game, the teams take a 10-minute rest and switch sides of the court for the second half.

In men's basketball, a team with the ball must advance it into the opponents' half of the court within ten seconds in American basketball and eight seconds in international competition. There is no ten-second rule in women's basketball. At all levels of men's and women's basketball, a player cannot be in possession of the ball for more than a certain number of seconds without taking a shot. This varies from 24 seconds in the professional and international leagues to 35 seconds in colleges. Attacking players cannot stay in the 'key' area for more than three consecutive seconds.

In order to score three points a player must be at least 6.25 m from the basket. This distance is marked by a semi-circular 'three-point line', shown here in white.

Then and now fact

Basketball was originally played with a soccer ball. This would have been a size of between 68 and 70 cm (27 and 28 inches) in circumference and a weight of about 450 g (16 oz). Today, a regular basketball is between 74.9 and 76.2 cm (29.5 to 30 inches) in circumference and weighs 567 to 624 g (20 to 22 oz).

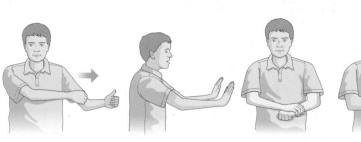

| charging | pushing | holding | blocking | technical foul | unsportsmanlike or flagrant foul. This can lead to player's ejection from the game. |

When a foul occurs in a game, referees blow their whistles, which stops play. They then use hand signals and body motions to indicate the offence. Some of the most common foul signals are shown in the illustrations above.

The court

Whether indoors or outside, basketball is played on a rectangular court. At each end, 3.05 metres above the court, are baskets 45 centimetres wide attached to backboards. The four-sided lined rectangular area under the basket is known as the 'key' or 'post'. The **free-throw** line, from which players shoot foul shots (penalties) after a **personal foul**, is 4.6 metres from the line at the end of the court. The arc that curves outside the key at each end is called the three-point line. Scoring shots from behind that line count for three points rather than the standard two.

Fouling

A player who brushes, touches or strikes the arm or hand of a player who is in the act of shooting is judged to have committed a **foul**. Depending on the situation, the shooter is awarded one, two or three free throws. A player who is hit while shooting but still makes the shot, is awarded the points plus one free throw. If the shot was a missed two-point attempt, the player is awarded two free throws. A player who is fouled and misses a three-point shot is awarded three free throws.

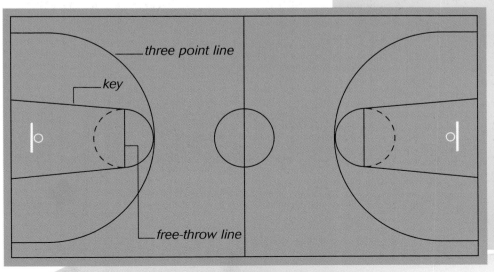

three point line

key

free-throw line

Basketball courts in the NBA, American college basketball (NCAA) and in international play (FIBA) are the same size: 28 metres long and 15 metres wide. However there are several differences between the courts. One of these is the width of the three point arc which is 7.24 metres in NBA basketball, 6.25 metres in FIBA and 6.02 metres in NCAA.

Coaching

Any athlete who decides to try out for a basketball team must impress the coach. They are the men and women who choose and teach the people who will play for them. No matter what talent level their players exhibit, all coaches look for the following qualities in players.

Discipline

It is a coach's job to point out weak points and offer tips on how to improve. A disciplined player will spend extra time working on his or her weak points.

For example, Latrell Sprewell of the Minneapolis Timberwolves was a poor **free-throw** shooter early in his career and now shoots an extra 200 free throws after every practice. He has become one of the most accurate free-throw shooters in the NBA.

Effort

A good coach motivates his or her team by pushing the players harder than they believe possible. Most coaches would rather have an average player who tries hard than a talented player who is lazy.

In 1947, the UCLA men's college basketball team finished last in its league. But in 1948 the same team, under coach John Wooden, won 22 games. Wooden claimed that his players were not as talented as other teams, but 'they led the league in hustle (attitude)'.

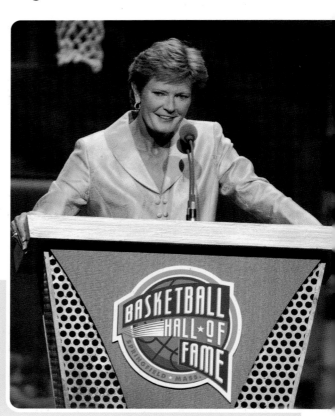

Pat Summit

University of Tennessee women's coach Pat Summit has won six national championships. She is a fierce competitor but insists that her players:

- maintain self-control at all times
- show respect for officials and opposing team members
- acknowledge superior skills in other players
- understand and appreciate the rules of the game.

Coaches look for skilled players who possess qualities such as self-discipline and sportsmanship. Talent is important but talent alone will not create a winning team. Coaches want players who can take criticism and use it to improve their play. Here Spanish coach Vincente Rodriguez instructs his team during the Women's European Championship in Amalidia, Greece, in 2003.

The Wizard of Westwood

John Wooden is widely recognized as the greatest coach in the history of American college basketball. In his 27 years as the coach at the University of California at Los Angeles (UCLA), located in the suburb of Westwood, his teams compiled a record of 620 wins against 147 losses. His team set the collegiate record of 88 consecutive victories. Throughout his long career, Wooden was often asked about the secret of his unmatched success. Here are some of the things he has said about the art and science of coaching basketball.

'Do not let what you cannot do interfere with what you can do.'

'You must have respect … for those under your supervision. Then they will do what you ask and more.'

'Perfection is an impossibility but striving for perfection is not. Do the best you can. That is what counts.'

Nutrition for athletes

Athletes should always consider the purpose of the food they eat and when they eat it. Protein foods such as meat or beans, for example, are necessary for the development of muscles and bones, but provide little in terms of energy. Thus a high protein meal before practice or a game will not provide the necessary fuel for the body. That is the role of carbohydrates such as pasta, rice or bread.

Daily diet

Young people who are involved in strenuous athletic activities such as basketball generally need to consume more food than children who are inactive.

Nutrition experts say it is important for athletes to eat regularly. Skipping meals, especially breakfast, takes a toll on athletic performance.

Essential foods

An athlete should aim to eat several servings of carbohydrates such as pasta, rice, bread and cereal during the day. Carbohydrates fuel the body and a lack of them in the diet can cause even the most skilled athlete to fade as a game wears on.

Along with carbohydrates, nutritionists recommend several servings of fruits and vegetables per day. These foods provide vital vitamins and minerals that keep the body 'machine' running smoothly.

A balanced diet of proteins and carbohydrates and at least five servings of fruit and vegetables is essential for a healthy diet.

Bananas contain large amounts of potassium which is excreted when an athlete sweats. A lack of potassium can lead to cramps so bananas should be a regular part of the diet.

Game day nutrition

A pre-game meal should fuel players, but leave them feeling comfortable for the game. Game-day meals should be based on carbohydrates and exclude excessive fat and protein that take longer to digest.

- 3+ hours before: peanut butter, lean meat, low-fat cheese or yogurt, a baked potato, cereal with low-fat milk or pasta with tomato sauce.

- 2–3 hours before: carbohydrates such as bread. Fats like butter should not be spread on these items as they can upset the stomach during exercise.

UK star Chris Haslam drinks water during a break in game action. Hydration is crucial before, during and after a game.

- 1–2 hours before: fruits such as bananas, melons and peaches are good choices. Nothing should be eaten less than an hour before a game or strenuous practice, so the body uses its energy to play for the game, not to digest food.

- Post-game recovery snacks may include sports drinks, liquid meal supplements, fruit, sandwiches and cereal bars.

Hydration fact

Athletes of all ages must drink fluids throughout the day, and it is critically important during a period of intense physical activity. Coaches generally recommend at least one cup of water or mineral-enhanced sports drink for every half-hour of activity.

Running

Fitness experts claim that playing a basketball game is equal to running 8 kilometres (5 miles) at top speed. In order to perform well, players have to be in excellent physical condition. The most important aspect of that conditioning is the cardiovascular system – the heart and lungs.

Shaping up

Basketball is a game of running, jumping, speed and coordination. Coaches agree that the best way to get in 'basketball' shape is to set up a regular schedule of distance running. Running several kilometres at a moderate pace will build what coaches call a fitness base. Many basketball training programmes require players to do such distance running in the off-season, in order to begin the season in shape.

Basketball is a sport of all-out running. Players who cannot keep up with the pace will generally lose. Teams often warm up before a game by jogging up and down the court and working up to all-out sprints.

Once regular practices begin, coaches at the most successful programmes begin and end sessions with **wind sprints** in which players race up and down the court. To make the sprints similar to game conditions, some coaches make players sprint one way then stop, turn and sprint the other way, just as they would in a game. Coaches can usually tell when a player is out of shape if he or she leans over with hands on knees between sprints. Fit players should be panting, but standing straight and ready to run again.

Coordination and conditioning

Basketball not only requires a healthy cardiovascular system, it also demands coordination. One of the best ways to mix conditioning and coordination is skipping. Spending ten to fifteen minutes several times a week can improve coordination and develop a player's leg muscles and ankles. Most coaches agree that good jump shooters need strong legs to give height and distance to their shots. Skipping, they say, helps to build a solid shooting foundation.

During practice sessions, coaches generally try to find exercises that build basketball skills as well as fitness. One of the most commonly used workouts for conditioning and coordination is simply substituting straight out sprints with sliding the feet from side to side or running backwards. Both of these moves are required during games to play defence against an opponent.

For sliding side-to-side, they move one foot until it touches the other, then slide that foot out. For sprinting backwards, players take short, quick strides while running backwards.

Skipping is an excellent conditioning exercise for basketball. It develops the lungs as well as the muscles in the legs used for jumping.

Aerobic and anaerobic fact

Aerobic means 'with oxygen' and refers to exercise that increases the heart rate, which forces oxygen into the bloodstream. The better-conditioned an athlete is, the more oxygen they breathe in and the more carbon dioxide waste they breathe out.

Anaerobic (without oxygen) activity such as sprinting requires an athlete to take in more oxygen than is possible to fuel the heart and lungs. This imbalance causes carbon dioxide to build up causing cramps and extreme fatigue. The fitter a person is, the longer it takes to reach the imbalance. Thus, anaerobic conditioning — like wind sprints — is a key part of conditioning in basketball.

Flexibility

Basketball requires athletes to have loose, flexible muscles for jumping, twisting, passing, shooting and other actions. Flexibility exercises are part of every top athlete's workout, practice or pre-game activity.

Warm up

Flexibility is the main goal of the warm up before any activity. A good warm up begins with a light jog that increases the heart beat and breathing. This in turn increases blood flow to the muscles that will soon be in use. Muscles that are ready to work tend to be more resilient against injury. Many teams jog laps around the court until the players are perspiring and panting slightly. At that point, the muscles are ready for stretches.

Stretches

Fitness experts say the key to stretching is to work on the largest muscles first. Athletes should not bounce during stretches, instead, a stretch should be done in a slow, controlled manner. Exhaling to begin the stretch, then breathing normally through the stretch works best. Experts recommend holding each stretch for 20 to 30 seconds.

Stretches might feel slightly uncomfortable, but should never be painful. An athlete should feel the stretch in the muscles, not the knees, elbows, hips or other joints.

Stretches should always be performed for both sides of the body as well as each limb.

A regular part of a pre-game stretch is a twist that loosens the large muscles in the lower back. These muscles often become tight due to constant running and jumping.

Hamstring stretch

Position: Back on the floor with one leg bent and one leg straight. Fingers interlocked behind thigh.

Stretch: Lift bent leg towards ceiling, pulling with hands, and hold for 15–20 seconds. Repeat twice on each leg.

Calf stretch

Position: Arms extended against a wall with rear leg straight, heel flat on the ground.

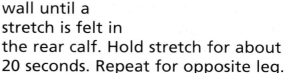

Stretch: Slowly lean into the wall until a stretch is felt in the rear calf. Hold stretch for about 20 seconds. Repeat for opposite leg.

Quadriceps stretch

Position: Standing with one hand against support for balance.

Stretch: Grab ankle with other hand and gently pull toward buttocks. Hold for 20–25 seconds. Repeat exercise with other leg.

Flexibility after an injury

Ankle sprains are common among basketball players at every level. Pro player Troy Murphy of the Golden State Warriors sprained an ankle in the 2002 season when he stepped on an opposing player's foot and rolled his ankle joint over. After doctors made certain there was no fracture in the ankle he was given a series of exercises to regain strength and flexibility in his ankle.

Although hobbling at the end of the 2002–03 season, Murphy had returned to full strength by the following season.

Basketball fitness – strength

Basketball players need to build strength in their arms, hands and legs to help in shooting, passing and jumping. At one time coaches were concerned that players who lifted weights would become muscle-bound – unable to move freely on the court. Today, most coaches believe strength training helps players avoid injury and increases their stamina. Players are more muscular than they have been in the past, but by combining strength with flexibility exercises, their movements are not limited.

The right exercise

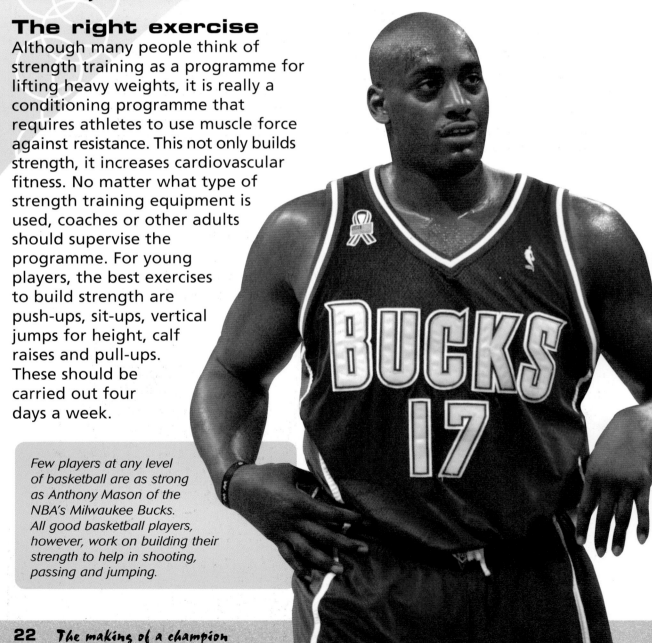

Although many people think of strength training as a programme for lifting heavy weights, it is really a conditioning programme that requires athletes to use muscle force against resistance. This not only builds strength, it increases cardiovascular fitness. No matter what type of strength training equipment is used, coaches or other adults should supervise the programme. For young players, the best exercises to build strength are push-ups, sit-ups, vertical jumps for height, calf raises and pull-ups. These should be carried out four days a week.

Few players at any level of basketball are as strong as Anthony Mason of the NBA's Milwaukee Bucks. All good basketball players, however, work on building their strength to help in shooting, passing and jumping.

Pull-ups

Pull-ups are an excellent exercise to build basketball muscles in the shoulders, chest and upper arms. To do a pull-up, an athlete first positions a bar several inches above his or her outstretched arms. The player jumps up to grasp the bar with both hands facing away from the body at shoulder width. The player then pulls his chin up to the bar (pull-ups are also called chin-ups) as many times as possible.

Australian Shane 'Hammer' Heal, who played in three Olympics as well as in the NBA, did 40 pull-ups in his workouts for the NBA's Minnesota Timberwolves. He played a season for the team and his great strength allowed him to make shots from far beyond the three-point line.

Shane 'Hammer' Heal who played in three Olympics as well as in the NBA for the NBA's Minnesota Timberwolves is renowned for his strength. His powerful arms allow him to make shots from far beyond the three-point line.

Women and weights

Although weight-lifting and other forms of strength training have come into wide use in men's basketball in the past 20 years, such training only entered women's basketball in the past decade. Since its introduction, strength training has been shown to provide great benefits for female athletes. Those benefits include increased speed, endurance, physical strength and a higher self-confidence. Strength training by women also aids in rehabilitation and recovery. One of the best ways to heal many types of injuries is to strengthen muscles surrounding the injured area. The stronger the muscles, the quicker the healing process.

Fitness experts say that strength training should be done only under close supervision. They also agree that female athletes gain the most benefit from many repetitions of lifting light to moderate weights.

Injuries and recovery

All players should wear safety equipment such as mouth guards, knee pads and sports eyewear if necessary. Even so, anyone can suffer injuries in a basketball game. The most frequent injury occurs in areas of the body where the muscles and bones are joined by tendons and ligaments.

Connecting tissue

Muscles are connected to the bones by tendons, which are cords of tough tissue. Ligaments are connective tissue that hold bones together at joints. They are found particularly in ankles, shoulders and knee joints.

The most common basketball injuries are ligament sprains and tendonitis. The most commonly injured areas of a basketball player's body are the ankles, knees and fingers.

Ankle injuries

More than one-third of all injuries in basketball are ankle sprains. The best way for athletes to prevent ankle sprains is to make sure that shoes are tightly laced around the ankle. Ankle injury can be prevented with strengthening exercises, pre-game stretching, and the use of ankle braces to support the joint.

Knee injuries

The knee is the largest joint in the human body. The anterior cruciate ligament, or ACL, is the ligament most often injured by common basketball moves. Many basketball players who suffer from knee pain are usually suffering from tendonitis, which occurs from overuse of the knee's patellar tendon that connects the knee cap (patella) to the shin bone (tibia). Called 'jumper's knee', patellar tendonitis may cause sharp pain during exercise activity and a throbbing ache off the court.

Basketball places a great deal of stress on the ligaments in the knee. The ligaments must straighten to hold the knee in place when it is in extension – that is, extended straight, as in jumping. The ligaments must also contract to allow freedom of motion when the knee is in flexion – that is, bent, as in running.

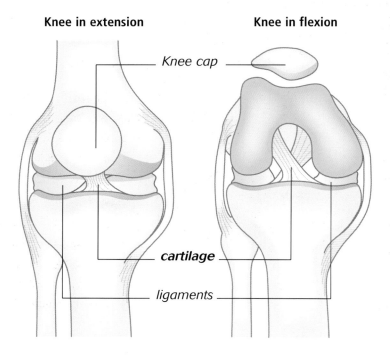

Knee in extension   **Knee in flexion**

Knee cap

cartilage

ligaments

The ankle is one of the most commonly injured joints among both men and women basketball players. The twisting and jumping that the sport requires place heavy demands on the ligaments that connect the foot with the lower leg.

Finger injuries

Sprained or 'jammed' fingers are usually caused by being hit on the tip of the finger by the ball or another player. Athletes are often reluctant to treat these injuries because it is 'just a finger'. Nevertheless, finger injuries, like ankle sprains, can recur unless they are treated properly.

For treatment of injuries such as sprains, athletic trainers recommend that athletes remember the initials RICE:

Rest: Stop playing.

Ice: Keep an ice pack on the injured area for the first 24 hours, alternating fifteen minutes with ice and fifteen minutes without ice.

Compression: After the 24 hours, wrap a bandage around the injured area – keep it tight but not so tight that it will cut off circulation.

Elevation: Keep the injured area raised during the first 24–48 hours after injury to prevent blood flow to the area.

Sue Bird

Sue Bird of the Seattle Storm is one of the most famous players in women's professional basketball. However, in 1998, she badly damaged the ACL in her left knee. She had major knee surgery in December 1998 and missed the rest of her season as a college player.

It took nearly a year of strenuous rehabilitation to repair her knee, but in 2000, she led her team, the Lady Huskies of Connecticut, to win the national title. In 2002, she was named the Women's US National Basketball Player of the Year.

Skills – dribbling

Dribbling a basketball is a critical skill for all players, yet dribbling well takes concentration and practice to master. Two things separate a good dribbler from a mediocre one: the ability to use both hands and the ability to dribble without looking at the ball. One of the best dribblers in pro basketball is Canadian point guard Steve Nash of the NBA Dallas Mavericks. Watching him in action illustrates one of the most important points of dribbling. He dribbles the ball using the fingertips, not the palms of his hands.

The basics

Good dribblers keep their head erect in order to see the entire court. To dribble, a player should have their arm hanging straight down with the upper arm close to the upper body. The elbow should be bent, allowing the upper arm to move up slightly as the fingertips receive the ball. When wrist and fingertips push the ball down, the bent elbow straightens. The wrist and elbow joints are relaxed during dribbling. The lower a player dribbles, the easier it is to do so by touch. A player should not dribble a ball higher than his or her waist. Placing the hand underneath or on the side of the ball while dribbling is an offence known as carrying or palming. A player who 'carries' the ball will lose possession.

Troy Parker shows perfect dribbling technique, keeping his body close to the ground.

Then and now

Perhaps the most important difference between basketball today and the sport played in the early years is that in the past there was no rule for the most common method of handling a basketball – dribbling. Dribbling actually developed several years after the first game was played. Early players realized that one way around the rule that prohibited running with the ball was to temporarily lose possession of it. Crafty players soon rolled it or bounced it on the floor as they moved toward the goal. One bounce led to another, and eventually players were running up the court while bouncing the ball. James Naismith, the founder of basketball, was delighted with the new technique. He called the dribble 'one of the most spectacular and exciting manoeuvres in basketball'.

Dribbling hints

To become a good dribbler:

- learn to dribble the ball equally well with either hand

- keep the knees bent while dribbling

- avoid looking at the ball

- avoid dribbling immediately upon receiving a pass. Assess your position on the court and decide whether a teammate is open for a pass

- don't try to show off

- practise daily.

Skills – passing

Learning to pass is one of the first skills to be mastered in basketball. Good players always pass with the fingertips and should pass to the receiver's chest, where the ball can be handled easily. Although she often makes flashy 'no-look' passes, Ticha Penicheiro, like all players, first mastered basketball's three basic passes: chest, bounce and overhead.

Chest pass

For a chest pass, the thumbs should be at the back of the ball pointing upward and the fingers around the sides of the ball. A passer steps into the pass and snaps the wrists, with the thumbs extending towards the receiver. The passer should complete the pass with the thumbs pointing downwards on the follow-through.

Bounce pass

Because a bounce pass is pushed down to the floor and bounces up to the pass receiver, the ball can sometimes make its way through the arms and legs of closely bunched defenders.

It is important for the passer to know how far from the receiver the ball should strike the floor. If it strikes too far away, the ball will float into the air and be easily intercepted. If the ball strikes the floor too close to the receiver, it will be more difficult to handle.

An accurate bounce pass should hit the floor about three-quarters of the way to the receiver. As with the chest pass, a passer should step into the pass and snap the wrists, moving the thumbs through the ball and towards the receiver.

A chest pass is thrown with the fingertips, while the thumbs face the passer. Mohamed Hachad demonstrates this during the Big Ten Men's Basketball Tournament in March 2003 in Chicago, Illinois.

The overhead pass

Throwing the ball a long distance requires strong wrist and upper arm action. In the two-hand overhead pass, a passer must throw the ball in an arc rather than a straight line to make it travel further. The arc should be just enough to get over the extended hands of a defender.

Ray Young of the UCLA Bruins performs an overhead pass during a game against the USC Trojans in Los Angeles, California.

Ticha Penicheiro

Patricia 'Ticha' Penicheiro is widely considered the best passer in women's professional basketball. The mark of a good passer is the number of assists – passes that lead directly to baskets – they can claim. Penicheiro has led the WNBA in assists for five consecutive seasons. She also set the league record for assists in a game, with 16 against the Los Angeles Sparks in 2003.

Born in Portugal, the 1.8 metres-tall Penicheiro was a member of the Portuguese national team and represented her country for the first time when she was just 14, playing in the 1988 Olympic Games. In 1993, she came to the USA to further her education before joining the Womens' National Basketball Association (WNBA) in 1998. She now plays for the Sacramento Monarchs.

Skills – shooting

Putting the ball in the basket is the object of the game of basketball, and shooting is the only way to accomplish that objective. Besides the dunk – which is only for the tallest players – the only other shots are the **lay-up**, the jump shot and the **free-throw**.

Two of the best shooters in basketball are Dirk Nowitzki from Germany who plays for the NBA's Dallas Mavericks, and Lauren Jackson from Australia who plays for the WNBA's Seattle Storm. Both Nowitzki and Jackson can make all three shots, but it is their jump shots that make them dangerous to opponents.

The lay-up

The lay-up is the easiest shot and the first shot all players should master since it is taken close to the basket. A player aims to bounce the ball off the backboard. Young players should push the ball up with two hands aiming for a point slightly off centre in the box above the rim. It is very important to be able to shoot a lay-up with either hand.

Jump shots

For a jump shot, players hold the ball above and in front of the head. In one motion, they raise the ball and rotate the shooting hand behind and under it. The non-shooting hand slides slightly under the ball to help guide the ball.

Good shooters have only a slight bend in the elbow of the shooting arm. The forearm is vertical and the wrist is directly over the elbow. The index finger of the shooting hand is pointed towards the basket.

WNBA great Sheryl Swoopes shows perfect form as she lets the ball roll off her finger for a lay-up shot.

Lauren Jackson

At 1.96 metres tall, Lauren Jackson is one of the tallest players in women's basketball. Her deadly shooting accuracy makes her one of the WNBA's premier players. By 2001, Jackson had played in more than 60 international games with Australia's national team, the Opals. In 1997, Jackson became the youngest member ever selected for the Australian women's national basketball team. At 17, she averaged 11 points as her team captured the bronze medal at the 1998 World Championships. In 2003, she became the youngest player in WNBA history to reach 1000 career points on 3 June, at 22 years and 27 days old. Jackson now plays for Seattle Storm.

The jump is an upward thrust by both legs. At the high point of the jump, the ball is released by extending the elbow and pushing the forearm and wrist. The wrist should snap completely forwards to follow through.

Free-throws

Free-throws can make all the difference between winning and losing a game. All good free-throw shooters follow the same routine. They line up the foot that is the opposite of the shooting hand – right-handed shooters use the left foot – with the centre mark of the free-throw line. They aim towards the front of the rim and shoot the ball at that point with an arc. A ball that hits the rim generally rolls in.

Even as a young player in Germany, NBA star Dirk Nowitzki of the Dallas Mavericks had perfect form on his jump shot. All good jump shooters like Nowitzki face the basket with their shoulders squared. They shoot from a balanced position and jump straight up. Accurate shooters rarely fall forwards, sideways or backwards after a shot.

Attack

As a player attacks the defending team, the object is to put the ball into the basket. But even players without the ball can help their team by moving on the court. Nothing frustrates coaches more than players who simply stand still.

Keep moving

Most coaches teach players without the ball to do the following:

- move into an open spot on the floor for a pass

- maintain distance of at least four to five metres between teammates

- watch the ball and be alert for a quick pass

- when a teammate takes a shot, get into position to grab the rebound if it misses

- be prepared to help a teammate who is trapped by a defender.

There are two important ways that players without the ball can help a team.

Screening

A screen or 'pick' occurs when an attacking player steps between a defensive player and the player she is **guarding**. This gives the player with the ball a clear look at the basket. Under basketball rules, once a **screener** has set her feet in position, she cannot move. Thus, a screener must stand firmly to avoid being bumped and moved.

Faking

Faking is also an important skill that can help a player get free for an open pass or easy shot. Good passers, for example, fake defenders by looking the opposite way to where they intend to pass.

Mike Brown of Brighton has attacked the basket and drawn two defenders to guard him. In response, he 'wraps' a pass around the leaping defender to his right, directing the ball to an open teammate.

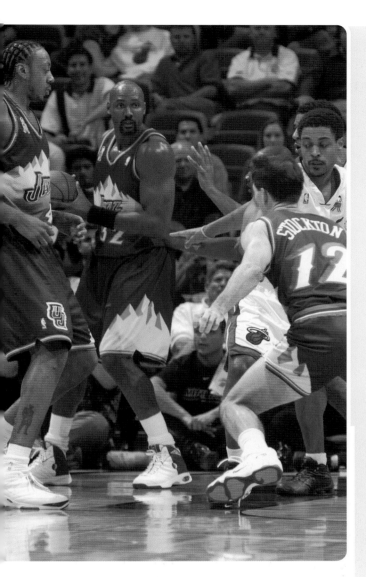

Stockton and Malone

Although the pick-and-roll has been used almost since basketball's earliest days, it was perfected in recent years by two of the greatest players in NBA history, John Stockton and Karl Malone (facing the camera) of the Utah Jazz. The relationship between the two men is legendary in basketball history. Stockton, a 1.8 metres-tall guard is from the northwest state of Washington while the 2 metres-plus Malone, is from the southern state of Louisiana. The two men had little in common except a burning desire to excel on the basketball court.

For 18 years, the two teammates defined basketball excellence. Although they never won an NBA championship, they led the Jazz to the **NBA playoffs** for a record eighteen straight years. The two men were teammates and gold medal winners on the 1992 US Olympic 'Dream Team'. The duo shared the **Most Valuable Player** award at the 1993 **NBA All-Star Game**. Both men were chosen among the 50 greatest basketball players of all time.

Players without the ball can get free from their defender in the same way by moving their eyes opposite to the way they will go. Players can also deceive their opponents by making a quick step in one direction then moving swiftly in the opposite direction.

The pick-and-roll

The pick-and-roll is a traditional basketball move done by two players, one with the ball and one without. The execution of the pick-and-roll, also called the screen-and-roll, begins when an attacking player, often a forward, sets a screen. The player with the ball, often a **guard**, drives directly towards the pick, attempting to draw the defender around the screener. The moment the defender moves towards the dribbler, the screener cuts ('rolls') towards the basket and takes a pass from a teammate for an open shot.

Transition

Basketball is a fast-moving game, one that requires players to switch from attack to defence and vice versa. This phase of the game is called **transition**. One of the most effective ways for a team to switch quickly from defence to attack is the **fast break**. The fast break requires speed and good ballhandling skills. If the fast break is done well, it is one of the most exciting moves in basketball and it involves the participation of every player on the team.

Centre

The fast break begins when the centre – a tall player such as Tim Duncan of the San Antonio Spurs – grabs an opponent's missed shot. The moment other players see that their big man has the ball, they sprint down the court. The ball is passed to the best ballhandler, usually a **guard** running down the centre of the court. The big player then trails the faster players up the court, usually in the centre lane.

Guards

Guards, like Ray Allen of the NBA's Seattle Supersonics, usually control the fast break. A guard must keep his or her head up during the fast break. By the time the guard reaches the three point arc, he or she must decide what to do with the ball. If there is no defender **blocking** the lane to the basket, the guard goes in for a **lay-up**. If a defender is there, he or she can pass to other players sprinting down the court.

Forwards

In most cases, **forwards**, such as Andrew Gaze of the Australian national team, are the players who

Big, fast forwards such as Elton Brand of the Los Angeles Clippers often dunk the ball at the end of a fast break.

shoot the ball at the end of the fast break. They must beat their defender down the court, so they will have a clear path to the basket if they receive a pass. They should keep their hands up, to make it easier for the guard to see them. Once the ball is in the forward's hand, he or she can shoot or **fake** the shot and pass to an unmarked teammate. Some forwards may flip the ball to the centre, who is trailing the play and is often forgotten by defenders who have raced back down the court.

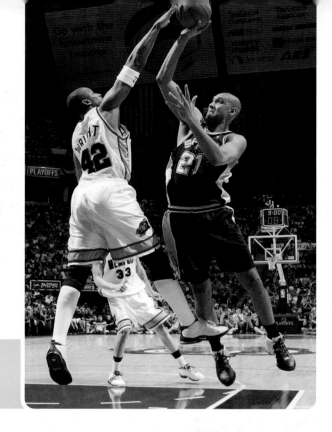

Tim Duncan (right) of the San Antonio Spurs, has his shot blocked. He now will have to defend against his opponent. This is called transition.

Jason Kidd – master of the fast break

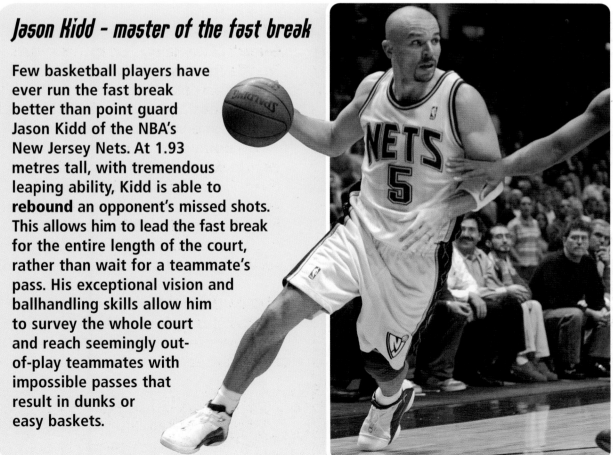

Few basketball players have ever run the fast break better than point guard Jason Kidd of the NBA's New Jersey Nets. At 1.93 metres tall, with tremendous leaping ability, Kidd is able to **rebound** an opponent's missed shots. This allows him to lead the fast break for the entire length of the court, rather than wait for a teammate's pass. His exceptional vision and ballhandling skills allow him to survey the whole court and reach seemingly out-of-play teammates with impossible passes that result in dunks or easy baskets.

Getting position

Most successful teams are not only good at attacking, they are strong defensively. The main job of a defender is to protect the area closest to the basket, where scoring is easiest for an attacking player. To achieve this goal, teams must work to make sure that opponents do not get **fast break** baskets. They also try hard to disrupt opponents' **cuts**, **drives** and passes.

Defensive stance

Experienced players agree that good defence begins with good footwork. Just as good shooters have a position that allows accurate shooting, defenders have a stance that enables them to react quickly. Good defenders lean forward slightly, with knees bent, and their weight on the balls of the feet. This way they are prepared for quick movement in any direction.

Scouting opponents

Good defenders always scout their opponents. Sometimes they have played the opponent before. Other times they watch opponents in warm-ups to see whether a player feels he is a better dribbler or shooter with the right or left hand. With that knowledge, a defender can force that player to use the weaker hand.

Taking a charge

In basketball, it is illegal for an attacking player to push into a defender who has his or her feet firmly planted. A player who does so is called for a **charge** and loses possession of the ball. Good defenders will often 'take a charge' and allow themselves to be bowled over if it means their opponent loses the ball. But this can be a gamble. Officials who see even the slightest movement of the defender into the player with

A good defender uses his hands to reach for the ball or to obstruct the vision of the opponent. No contact is permitted between the defender's hand and the opponent's body.

the ball may call blocking, a defender's **foul**. To make certain to get a charging call, a good defender always follows these steps:

- plants their feet before the attacking player arrives

- does not move before the attacking player hits them

- yells when they get hit to convince the official that the attacking player charged.

This defender is not moving his feet quickly enough to stop Dirk Nowitzki from getting past him.

The all round game of Michael Jordan

Most basketball fans agree that Michael Jordan, pictured below, was one of – if not the – greatest players ever to play basketball. The Chicago Bulls teams of the 1990s won six NBA championships with Jordan as their captain and leader. Amazingly, Jordan was dropped from his high school team because he was not a good defender. After that snub, Jordan worked as hard on his defence as he did on his shooting and passing. In practice, he often played defence with his hands behind his back. This forced him to concentrate on moving his feet instead of reaching with his hands. In games, that footwork enabled him to slide and back pedal in order to keep his opponent in front of him.

Game day

One of the most successful basketball teams in the USA in recent years has been the University of Connecticut women's basketball team. The UCONN Lady Huskies won four national collegiate championships between 1995 and 2003. Head coach Geno Auriemma, assistant head coach Chris Dailey, and two assistant coaches Tanya Cardoza and Jamelle Elliot all have specific jobs on game day. A typical game day begins with a pre-game meal about three hours before the match. From that point, the team's activities run according to a very precise schedule which is detailed below.

Two hours till tip-off

Players who require special taping of their hands have that done. Others may receive treatment for minor injuries. Most players go through pre-game rituals that help them prepare mentally for the game. Some listen to music. Others read or watch videos of their opponents.

One hour till tip-off

All players are in their team kit. On court they stretch and take **free-throws** to make sure their eyes are adjusted to the background behind the basket. Others practise shots from certain spots on the court. They prepare themselves to take that shot if they get the ball during the game.

Coaches remind players of opposing players who need special attention. They also make notes about which players will start the game and who will be the first substitutes during the game.

UCONN coach Geno Auriemma gives some advice and encouragement to captain Diana Taurasi during a game.

Thirty minutes till tip-off

Once individual warm-ups have finished, the players begin organized passing and shooting drills. While players break into a light sweat, coaches walk to the opponents' bench to shake hands with the opposing coaches and to discuss any concerns about the condition of the court or the actions of fans. Coaches from both teams meet the referees.

Ten minutes till tip off

With ten minutes to go until game time, the Lady Huskies leave the court and return to the locker room for the pre-game team talk. UCONN's coaches prefer a quiet time right before tip-off to focus players on the game. The starting line-up is announced. Defensive assignments are explained and attacking strategies are reviewed. Coaches remind players to move without the ball, set **screens**, and make passes crisp. They remind the players to keep calm and avoid turning the ball over to an opponent through careless ballhandling.

With a minute to go until tip-off, crowds cheer the UCONN Lady Huskies as they jog on to the court. Many of the fans are unaware how much work the coaches and players have done before the game begins.

University of Tennessee guard Kara Lawson (left) attempts to drive past defender Ashley Battle (right) of the University of Connecticut in a 2003 women's college championship game.

Olympic dreams

For many athletes, the opportunity to represent their country in an Olympic basketball competition is the dream of a lifetime. Regardless of whether the team wins, any athlete who makes his or her country's Olympic basketball team has the heart of a champion.

The 2000 Olympics

In the 2000 Olympic Games in Sydney, Australia, no team showed more heart than the men's team from Lithuania. Against a team of NBA All-Stars from the USA, the Lithuanians sent a squad of young college-age players. The NBA All-Stars had never won by fewer than 20 points since 1992, but the Lithuanians defended fiercely. They also took accurate shots and they nearly achieved the greatest upset in Olympic history.

During the semi-finals, Lithuania's Sarunas Jasikevicius, scored 27 points for his team against the USA. With a minute left, Lithuania led the mighty 'Dream Team' by one point. Then, an exhausted Jasikevicius, who hadn't missed a **free-throw**, missed two out of three. Forty seconds later, with the USA up by three points, Jasikevicius made a lay-up, and the two teams were just one point apart.

The Lithuanians then **fouled** Jason Kidd, and he made only one of two free-throws with 9.4 seconds left. Jasikevicius attempted a three-point jump shot at the final buzzer but that fell short. The Lithuanians lost 85 to 83, but to many fans, these tough young players were the heroes of the Olympics.

The USA's Kevin Garnett blocks a shot from Lithuania's Darius Songaila (in white) from behind during the 2000 Olympics.

Paralympic Games

Many fans look past the Olympics to the summer Paralympic Games, the international competition for athletes with disabilities. Perhaps the most popular of all sports at the Paralympic Games is wheelchair basketball. The sport differs only in regard to ballhandling and fouls. For example, a player may push on the wheels of the wheelchair no more than twice, before dribbling, passing or shooting. A foul occurs when a player **blocks**, holds, pushes, **charges** or stops the progress of an opponent.

One nation has dominated wheelchair basketball recently. Canada boasts the gold medal-winning men's and women's teams. The Canadian Women's Wheelchair basketball team, in fact, has won more than 40 straight international games, and has won the gold medal in every Paralympic Games since 1988.

Tamika Catchings

Tamika Catchings is one of the best all-round players in women's basketball. Drafted by Indiana Fever in the 2001 WNBA Draft, Catchings won the 2002 WNBA **Rookie of the Year** award. In 2002 she helped lead the United States national team to a gold medal in the FIBA World Basketball Championships for women, held in China.

Few would dispute that Catchings (right), is an outstanding player. What makes her a champion is that she accomplished all of her success despite being born with a profound loss of hearing.

Off court, Catchings gives speeches to young people who are disabled, letting them know that it is still possible for them to achieve their goals.

Being a champion

Many basketball players are champions on and off the court. Some may not be famous players on winning teams, but to fans they are still champions. Two such players are Swin Cash of the USA and John Amaechi of the UK.

Female hero

When Swin Cash appeared at the International Auto Show in Detroit, Michigan in January 2004, she drew a huge crowd of admirers.
An All-American at the University of Connecticut, she played in their 2000 and 2002 national championship teams. In the spring of 2002, she was the second player selected in the professional draft. Her first season with the Detroit Shock was difficult – the team had the worst record in the league. Cash returned in 2003 determined to improve their play. That determination was rewarded when the Shock became the only team in the history of American professional sports to improve from the worst record to the championship in one season.

Cash is also an exemplary role model for young women today. She has a key role in the WNBA 'Mind, Body, Spirit' program that helps young girls develop good fitness habits and self-confidence. Each year she also sponsors a scholarship for a college student who, like herself, excels both on and off the basketball court.

Swin Cash holds the championship trophy awarded to the Detroit Shock after winning the WNBA championship in 2003.

Magic Meech

Slightly fewer than 350 players make the rosters of NBA teams each season. Therefore even an NBA player who rarely gets into a game is a champion. One player who is not well known to many NBA fans is John Amaechi. 'Meech' as he is known on the court, is the first citizen of the UK to play in the NBA.

Raised in Manchester, England, Meech's first sport was rugby. As a teenager, however, he grew too tall and turned instead to basketball. He was offered a scholarship to Penn State University in the USA. After graduating in 1995, he played for the Cleveland Cavaliers and was the first British player to start an NBA game. For the next three seasons, Meech played professionally in France, Italy, Greece and England before returning to the NBA in 1999 playing for the Orlando Magic. Meech was traded to the Utah Jazz in 2001 and then to the Houston Rockets. In 2004, he returned to Manchester to play for the Manchester Magic.

Amaechi was as serious a student as he was a basketball player. He received a college degree in psychology and is now pursuing a PhD in child psychology.

Although Amaechi might not be a famous NBA player, he is a hero to young admirers in the USA and the UK. 'I've seen many ups and downs in basketball,' he says. 'But the game in America made me much more positive.'

The best there ever was

Andrew Gaze has played in a record five Olympic Games and is the highest points scorer in Olympic history. Gaze has also played for Australia in four world championships and is the second highest points scorer in world championship history. In his homeland, Gaze has been named the NBL's **Most Valuable Player** seven times and has scored more points in the NBL than any other player. Gaze was rewarded for his contribution to basketball by being named as Australian flag bearer for the opening ceremony at the Sydney Olympics in 2000. Olympic teammate Shane Heal once said of Gaze: 'When Andrew finally retires people will say, there goes Andrew Gaze – the best there ever was.'

Records

Although basketball players are world famous for their individual talents, the measure of success is determined by team performance. The first World Championships of the Fédération Internationale de Basketball Amateur (FIBA) were held for men in 1950 and the first women's championship in 1953. Tournaments are now held every four years. Sixteen countries take part. The host country automatically qualifies. The other 15 entries emerge from qualifying tournaments in the FIBA's five zones: Africa, Asia, Europe, the Americas and Oceania.

Olympic winners				
Year	Gold	Final	Silver	Bronze
1980	Yugoslavia	86–77	Italy	Soviet Union 117, Spain 94
1984	USA	96–65	Spain	Yugoslavia 88, Canada 82
1988	Soviet Union	76–63	Yugoslavia	USA 78, Australia 49
1992	USA	117–85	Croatia	Lithuania 82, Soviet Union 78
1996	USA	95–69	Yugoslavia	Lithuania 80, Australia 74
2000	USA	85–75	France	Lithuania 89, Australia 71
2004	Argentina	84-69	Italy	USA 104, Lithuania 96

NBA post-season awards – last 20 years			
Most Valuable Player			
1980–81	Julius Erving, Philadelphia	1992–93	Charles Barkley, Phoenix
1981–82	Moses Malone, Houston	1993–94	Hakeem Olajuwon, Houston
1982–83	Moses Malone, Philadelphia	1994–95	David Robinson, San Antonio
1983–84	Larry Bird, Boston	1995–96	Michael Jordan, Chicago
1984–85	Larry Bird, Boston	1996–97	Karl Malone, Utah
1985–86	Larry Bird, Boston	1997–98	Michael Jordan, Chicago
1986–87	Magic Johnson, Los Angeles Lakers	1998–99	Karl Malone, Utah
1987–88	Michael Jordan, Chicago	1999–2000	Shaquille O'Neal, Los Angeles Lakers
1988–89	Magic Johnson, Los Angeles Lakers	2000–01	Allen Iverson, Philadelphia
1989–90	Magic Johnson, Los Angeles Lakers	2001–02	Tim Duncan, San Antonio
1990–91	Michael Jordan, Chicago	2002–03	Tim Duncan, San Antonio
1991–92	Michael Jordan, Chicago	2003–04	Kevin Garnett, Minnesota Timberwolves

Recent NBA Champions

Year	Team	Year	Team
1993–94	Houston Rockets	1999–00	Los Angeles Lakers
1994–95	Houston Rockets	2000–01	Los Angeles Lakers
1995–96	Chicago Bulls	2001–02	Los Angeles Lakers
1996–97	Chicago Bulls	2002–03	San Antonio Spurs
1997–98	Chicago Bulls	2003–04	Detroit Pistons
1998–99	San Antonio Spurs	2004-05	San Antonio Spurs

Men's Championship Results

Year	Gold	Silver	Bronze
1954	USA	Brazil	Philippines
1959	Brazil	USA	Chile
1963	Brazil	Yugoslavia	Soviet Union
1967	Soviet Union	Yugoslavia	Brazil
1970	Yugoslavia	Brazil	Soviet Union
1974	Soviet Union	Yugoslavia	USA
1978	Yugoslavia	Soviet Union	Brazil
1982	Soviet Union	USA	Yugoslavia
1986	USA	Soviet Union	Yugoslavia
1990	Yugoslavia	Soviet Union	USA
1994	USA	Russia	Croatia
1998	Yugoslavia	Russia	USA
2002	Yugoslavia	Argentina	Germany

Women's Championship Results

Year	Gold	Silver	Bronze
1957	USA	Soviet Union	Czechoslovakia
1959	Soviet Union	Bulgaria	Czechoslovakia
1964	Soviet Union	Czechoslovakia	Bulgaria
1967	Soviet Union	South Korea	Czechoslovakia
1971	Soviet Union	Czechoslovakia	Brazil
1975	Soviet Union	Japan	Czechoslovakia
1979	USA	South Korea	Canada
1983	Soviet Union	USA	China
1986	USA	Soviet Union	Canada
1990	USA	Yugoslavia	Cuba
1994	Brazil	China	USA
1998	USA	Russia	Australia
2002	USA	Russia	Australia

Glossary

blocking
the use of a defender's body position to illegally prevent an opponent's advance; the opposite of charging

cartilage
semi-transparent flexible tissue that is found in some joints, the nose, and the external ear

centre
Usually the tallest player on a basketball team, this person competes for the opening jump ball to start games and plays close to the basket on defense to block shots

cut
an abrupt change in direction, with or without the basketball, to elude an opponent

charging
an attacking foul which occurs when an attacking player runs into a defender whose feet are planted

defensive rebound
a rebound of an opponent's missed shot

drive
when a player with the ball moves quickly towards the basket

fake
a deceptive move to throw a defender off balance and allow an attacking player to shoot or receive a pass; players use their eyes, head or any other part of the body to trick an opponent

fast break
transition from defence to attack that begins with a defensive rebound by a player who immediately sends an outlet pass toward midcourt to his waiting teammates; these teammates can sprint to the basket and quickly shoot before enough opponents catch up to stop them

forwards
the two players on the court for a team who are usually smaller than the centre and bigger than the guards; often a team's highest scorers

foul
action by a player which breaks the rules and is penalized by a change in possession or a free-throw opportunity

free-throw
a shot taken from the free throw line after a personal foul

guarding
the act of following an opponent around the court to prevent him from getting close to the basket, taking an open shot or making an easy pass, while avoiding illegal contact

guards
the two players on each team who are the smallest on the court; they usually handle setting up moves and passing to teammates closer to the basket

lay-up or lay-in
a shot taken after driving to the basket by leaping up under the basket and using one hand to drop the ball directly into the basket (lay-in) or to bank the ball off the backboard into it (lay-up)

Most Valuable Player
the award given to the player in the NBA each year who is most important to his team's success

NBA All-Star Game
a game played in mid-season between the best players of the eastern and western divisions. The starting teams are selected by the vote of fans.

NBA playoffs
the system by which the NBA champion is determined. The playoffs begin with the best of five game playoffs between the top eight teams in the western and eastern divisions. The NBA champions are determined by a best of seven playoff between the western and eastern division champions.

personal foul
contact between players that may result in injury or provide one team with an unfair advantage; players may not push, hold, trip, hack, elbow, restrain or charge into an opponent

rebound
when a player grabs a ball that is coming off the rim or backboard after a shot attempt

Rookie of the Year
the award given to the best first-year player (known as a rookie) in the NBA each year

screen or screener
the offensive player who stands between a teammate and a defender to give his teammate the chance to take an open shot

transition
the shift from attack to defence

travelling
a floor violation when the ball handler takes too many steps without dribbling; also called walking

wind sprints
conditioning drills in which players run all out for short distances numerous times

Resources

Further reading

Basketball (Eyewitness Books), John Hareas (Dorling Kindersley Publishing, 2003)

Bounce Back, Sheryl Swoopes, Greg Brown and Doug Keith (Taylor Publishing Company, 2000)

Fast Breaks: She's Got Game, Michelle Smith (Scholastic, 2002)

Fast Breaks: WNBA Superstars, Molly Jackel and Joe Layden (Scholastic, 2002)

Fundamental Basketball, James Klinzing (Lerner Publications Company, 1999)

NBA Basketball Basics, Mark Vancil (Sterling Publications, 1995)

Useful websites and addresses

National Basketball Association websites
Canada: www.nba.com/canada
USA: www.nba.com
UK: www.nba.com/uk

Women's National Basketball Association website
USA: www.wnba.com

England Basketball Association
England Institute of Sport,
Coleridge Road, Sheffield, S9 5DA
Phone: 0870 7744225
www.englandbasketball.co.uk

Basketball Australia
P.O. Box 17, Regents Park BC
NSW 2143
www.basketball.net.au

International Wheelchair Basketball Federation
109–189 Watson Street, Winnipeg, Manitoba, R2P 2E1, Canada
Phone: 001-204-632-6475
Fax: 001-204-925-5929
www.iwbf.org

Fédération Internationale de Basketball – FIBA
8, Ch. de Blandonnet
1214 Vernier / Geneva
Switzerland
Email: info@fiba.com
www.fiba.com

USA Basketball
5465 Mark Dabling Boulevard
Colorado Springs, CO 80918-3842
www.usabasketball.com

Basketball New Zealand
P.O. Box 6052
Marion Square, Wellington
Phone: 04 498 5950
www.basketball.org.nz

Disclaimer

All the Internet addresses (URLs) given in this book were valid as at the time of going to press. However, due to the dynamic nature of the Internet, some addresses may have changed, or sites may have changed or ceased to exist since publication. While the author and Publishers regret any inconvenience this may cause readers, no responsibility for any such changes can be accepted by either the author or the Publishers.

Index